Book Writing secrets for beginners

Written by:

Yogita Warde

NOTION PRESS

India. Singapore. Malaysia.

ISBN xxx-x-xxxxx-xx-x

Writing books feels like an adventure,

A whole new joueny that you go through.

Contents

Introduction .... *xi*

Is it worth writing a book?........ *14*

Why wait for the idea?........ *20*

What does it take to write a book? *24*

Outline and structure of your first book........ *34*

Getting to start writing........ *45*

Writing like a Pro........ *51*

How to Edit Like a Pro? *79*

It's time Guy's........ *83*

Yogita Warde

An Author with Impeccable Thoughts and Vision

The growing modern world is making people do whatever they want. The value of writing has been given top priority in educating people.

Yogita Warde, a well-known author, and tremendous human being is gaining much fame due to her writing skills. A woman who encourages people to do better in their lives. She believes in the power of words. Destiny has already decided to award her with a successful writing career. Since her childhood, she got deeply fascinated by writers and authors. The author is from Madhya Pradesh, also known as the heart of India. A simple girl with a big dream from Shujalpur, a village in Madhya Pradesh.

Now, the author is known globally for her achievements. One of her masterpieces "Saahi& Sudheer" highlights the love story of two different people. It is a beautiful love story between an artist and a writer. After reading this book, people would

get a broader aspect and knowledge about how friendship can turn into a deep love story. Like all writers, look for the ultimate reward, the reward of appreciation from the readers.

Yogita Warde got motivated by the praises and appreciation of the readers of her first book. Then she decided to write more books to entertain, educate and help people know the better reality of life. Yogita was always interested to help the women suffering in the patriarchal society. With her second book "Diya", Yogita decided to aware society of various difficulties and obstacles faced by women due to inequality and myths. The "Postcard" is another beautiful work by a renowned author. Postcard throws light on the real sufferings and struggles of people daily. The postcard is one of the best works of author Yogita Warde. In her book, she tried to give a message to readers that "You will succeed when you decide to not give up". With her fourth book "Cooker ki Seeti", Yogita Warde brought an engrossing and enticing drama series for youngsters and people of all ages. The book contains 6 different types of dramas, and each gives a unique message to the readers. And her fifth book "Gulmohar" is a poetic masterpiece that invites readers to explore life through a unique and enchanting perspective. With the eloquence of a poet's soul, the author paints a vivid picture of existence, likening it to the serene mountains, cool breezes, boundless skies, innocent childhood, carefree birds in flight, and the vibrant colours of a rainbow. In this compilation of poems, the essence of life is poured into words to make an impact in your life.

Yogita Warde is one of her kind. She was awarded and honored with some reputable awards. She was honoured with "LitFest 2020 Author of the year". Not only praises and lauding, but the author also received the "Tagore commemorative honouree Award 2021" for her masterpiece "Diya". She has also received 'Global Leadership Excellence Award 2022' by Aesthetics International and IHIW- 'Woman Author of The Year - 2022' by MTTV together with Global Women Inspiration Award & conclave 2022 and UkiyotoLitAwards Q2'22 Women Writer of the Year for her book "Cooker ki Seeti". And very recently she was honoured with the Asian Literary Award 2022 (5th Global Leadership Summit) by Aesthetics international. Also, she recently received "The real super woman Award 2022" from Forever Stat India.

Yogita Warde is a brilliant author and woman. A woman who wants to remove the barriers coming between all her dreams. At such a young age, Yogita Warde is paving her way toward success.

Yogita Warde is blessed with family members and friends who support her in every situation. With her plucky attitude, she is willing to fight out any

challenges that stop her from reaching her goals. Now, Yogita Warde is the real inspiration for every woman looking for an independent future. Words are the most powerful weapon in this world and Yogita is the wordsmith in the writing world.

Introduction

Writing books feels like an adventure, a whole new journey that you go through. There are ups and downs and challenges to face, these whole new and exciting sets of challenges often lead us to the most satisfying thing of our life, our first finished draft of the book. Pinning down your first book can be overwhelming, and it comes with feelings like struggling to be disciplined, feeling uninspired, having self-doubt, and others. But once you work on it and publish it, you start to feel like you have achieved something and feel proud of your achievements.

To pin down your first book, whatever it is, novel, short story, life lessons, and others, an underlying plan is crucial. Especially, when you lack clarity about the topics and don't have any experience in the writing, you struggle to finalize the plan. So, if you dream about authoring a best-selling book, you must start with making a flexible plan and keep making improvements in the plan till you finish drafting the first rough draft of your book.

The whole process can be simplified with the guidance of someone who has done this before. Therefore, in this book, I have compiled all the best tips and tricks and shared my learnings to help you draft your first book without any inconvenience. Here, together with sharing my personal thoughts, difficulties faced, it has also shared the effective solutions to ensure that you won't be facing similar problems.

Before you start with the preparations, I want to share that I am proud and happy for you as you are committed to writing your book and learning new things. There will be days when you might feel defeated and burned out, but you must give yourself a deserved break when this happens and resume your journey after rejuvenating your mind. This way you will get to see things from a broader perspective and make yourself capable of sharing the essence of your thoughts in the well-framed sentences.

When I was researching for one of my books and suddenly started to feel clueless about making it outline, that's when I realized there's no quick guide that helps us with the step-by-step process and offer us with the instant solutions to write books. So, here I am with the quick guide for beginners to help them develop their writing skills and make the most out of your creative thinking patterns, overthinking or lessons you learned from life.

As the content of this guide progresses, we will guide you through writing your first draft from scratch and talk about how you can make an outline, prepare an action plan, improve writing skills and finish your draft faster. All the things I have shared helped me in the past and get the book's recognition on the national level. So, excited to write your first book and inspire people around you? Why wait more? Turn around the pages of the book to explore the effective information and start drafting your book today! Best of luck, Brave reader!

Chapter-1

Is it worth writing a book?

When you decide to put your thoughts on paper and try writing in brief about your feelings, you can empathize with someone, make them feel stronger and do a lot unintentionally. There can be various reasons to start writing, different things can motivate and inspire you to sit down and pour your feelings on paper, and trust me, once you start writing there's no going back.

Writing brings more clarity in your thoughts and writing your books fills you up with seamless confidence and makes you feel worthy. When you start to question yourself, is it worth writing a book? Am I doing it right? And if you search that question up, you will get unlimited reasons to write a book. But the one reason that inspires you to write, your reason and motivation, you must find that before starting drafting a book. So, find your 'why' and stick to that one impactful reason to write your book. Also, when you will be publishing your book, your readers not only learn and enjoy that book, they can connect with that reason and become curious to know more.

In conclusion when you start to write, you can have thousands of excuses like, topics, writing style, skills and lack of tools and others. But if you have aspiration to and you have figured out your 'why' of writing a book, you will be unstoppable.

Explore more about yourself

Not only do you get to share your thoughts effectively by writing, you explore so much about yourself in the process. You can discover new aspects of your personality and stretch your limits together with getting out of your comfort zone. If you continue to keep your thoughts to yourself, no matter how great they are, you might forget them, sooner or later. So why not write to grab on to your best opinions, thoughts and lessons by writing a book?

Make you feel accomplished

From writing your first draft to getting it published is a long process and requires effort and lots of thought. When you overcome all the challenges and get the job done, it is an accomplishment you will feel proud of. In the journey of writing a book, you will know how capable you are and all the self-doubts that you get in the beginning of the journey, start to vanish. Further, it will also be life having a constant thing in your life, that motivates you in tough times and gives you hope.

Why should teachers and doctors become published authors?

As you will move further in this book, you get to know that the process of writing a book can be simplified and everyone can write their book. No matter in which profession you are and what you are pursuing in your career, writing a book is always beneficial as it gives you more authority over the subject, in addition you get acknowledged.

With a well searched book, blended perfectly with personal experience, a doctor can help their patients, teachers can educate their students and a businessman or entrepreneur can promote and make people aware about their brand. So, it wouldn't be wise to say no to a win-win situation.

Time to upgrade yourself

When you work a 9-5, you hardly get any time to work on yourself. If we leave the 9-5 aside and see things from a broader perspective, once we pass the phase, we start to lose interest in learning and don't pay much attention to the things we are curious about. Therefore, you must consider writing a book and upgrade your knowledge about preferred things and subjects. Furthermore, when you start writing any story book, you see things from different perspectives and turn the spotlight on your hidden capabilities. The reason behind I have stated all of that is, I personally believe in receiving and knowing about the things I am unfamiliar with before pinning them down in my books.

Make the world a better place with your words

Isn't it fascinating how beautifully we are connected to each other, with all the experiences, yet we all are unique individuals? We all go through the same phases, dealing with the same challenges throughout our lives. So, when you share about your experiences and how you felt and overcame various circumstances, you can encourage others. Someone who stays far away from you, can learn from your experiences, and have hope that one day, it will all be alright. With the power of worlds, light up hope in their heart and make them feel like they are not alone.

Why not start now?

Ask yourself: "What am I lacking and why can't I start now?"

Once you start to question, you figure out what is stopping you and offer yourself with the opportunity to work on those things. Suppose you can't start now because you have a busy schedule,

how about writing 500 words in a day? You can't begin because you have no ideas, then why not just put your raw thoughts down then further connect the dots? Similarly, whatever the excuse you are using and hurdles you are facing can be solved with undivided attention and some effort. Furthermore, in the beginning it might feel like doing so much, but as you move forward, you enjoy the process and like being productive.

I was on the seventh heaven when I finished the draft of my first book and all the discipline, struggles were worth it. Lastly, I want to add that, when you start, don't think you have a lot to write and it's a ton of work, just focus on the moment. Like, just focus on the target you have decided for the day and don't rush. Setting a deadline is crucial but that doesn't mean you have to pressurize yourself. Hope you got your 'Why' to write and now you are prepared to follow the steps listed in this book. Just write down the reason you have selected before you turn the pages to read further.

Write the book because you can!

Or because

Why not?

Chapter-2

Why wait for the idea?

Having the topic or an idea that excites you is significant, because you will not feel monotonous while writing. The idea you have will inspire you to write, no matter what it is, a key learning, a story's plot, a concept, or some subject, an exciting one is important. It's normal if you might start to doubt your idea and feel unsure about the commitment of writing a whole book dedicated to that. But trust me, the idea of who has can never be not good enough, because it's yours and only you can find the right words and frame sentences that convey that idea.

✓ ***Does my idea have to be grand?***

This seems to be a misconception among many inspired writers that you must have something mind-blowing to share to write a book or your idea has to be great. But an impactful idea is as crucial as a mind-blowing one. We read interesting facts and forget them simultaneously as it is none of our use. When you read something impactful that connects with your daily life, it works like a sweet reminder. Therefore, you don't have to wait for the great grand idea to start writing your book. If you have something that can add value to your readers' life and you are interested in that particular idea, go ahead and pin that down.

Write! Write!

When you stick to your decision about writing, ideas will frequently come, but if you choose to just let them flow without doing anything and taking actions, you soon run out of ideas. So, when an idea strikes, work on it. It can come anywhere anytime, and it happens with all the writers. As for me, I just record that idea with random thoughts on my notepad, so that I can work on it afterwards.

Try doing the same, suppose you have a story idea, but you are too occupied to work on that, just put on the recorder and speak 10-12 seconds about that idea. Further, when you resume writing you can research and see if the idea is worth it or not. Just remember, not to jump into conclusion and declare the idea a failure before moving forward with the research.

Now, what to do if you wish to write a book, but neither you have an idea prepared nor any subject?

The simple answer is to explore, read, get to know yourself more and ask yourself what you are

interested in. You can start with reading books that interest you, finding the topics that interest you, shortlisting them. In addition, you can start writing, let's not think about the topics, just pick any that looks fascinating and start writing on that. Then, soon you will know what topic interests you the most and you will not get bored while knowing, researching, and writing about that. Please know that, there will be a time when your most favorite subject will start to feel less exciting, but you must stay disciplined and committed to ensure the desired results.

Now, you are all set to start!

Chapter-3

What does it take to write a book?

When you plan to do something that can add value to others' lives, you have to write things in such a manner that can catch the attention of people and hold it. Presenting things in a unique manner together with highlighting the idea you aim to share. With all the things going on in the journey of writing your own book, you may wonder what it takes to write a book and if you possess those essential skills or not. Before we dive deep in to explore the things, know that there's nothing that you cannot learn and master with proper practice.

Firstly, set all the things aside, work on your time management and discipline. Not only do you invest time in new skills with discipline, you can also master things quicker with consistent efforts. When you are frustrated, you may feel exhausted and think that you are strict on yourself because of all the discipline you practice. But it makes you more independent and confident. Furthermore, in writing discipline is something that can come overnight because some days you will also feel the writer's block that will make you run out of words.

The key is to be consistent with the timings you have decided, just sit down and write. It doesn't matter if once or twice, you are not satisfied with what you are writing. You always have the option to edit that later. So, be disciplined if you successfully want to finish the first draft of your book.

In addition, learn the best ways to express yourself. Often it happens that you fail to convey your ideas, or you select the wrong words that change the whole gist of the idea. No matter how brilliant your idea is, wrong word choice and the manner of presenting works as a game changer. If you have just started out, it's something that needs to be worked upon and practicing consistently is the only solution here.

To start learning to work on the formation of the sentences and presentation of ideas, read mindfully and notice the time that leaves you in awe and makes you introspect. Notice how things are presented and highlight the other similar lines. Apart from reading, you can also listen to the podcast, watch TED talks, and watch movies and start observing. Write down the lines that hits you harder, on the other hand note down the leanings. Once you make this a habit of observing, you will notice how subconsciously, you frame the better sentences and use the best word to enhance your writing style.

Knowing what to consider and work on before starting the book, can do wonders and make you feel more prepared and confident. Although it's up to you, you can work on these things before writing the book or in between the journey. Furthermore, here are a few more things that I want you to focus on, so keep surfing through the pages to explore!

- ***Feeling clueless can fuel your procrastination and give you more excuses. So, it would be best to go for guidance. Like you have made the right decision by picking up this book, you can also talk to someone personally and join writing classes that educate you about the best writing secrets and help you with some practice lessons.***

- ***Starting from having an idea and planning outline to deciding the sequence of final chapters, indeed it is going to be time consuming. Therefore, you must make flexible plans, outline, and avoid micro planning because that can be a headache in the long run. Flexible plans allow you to level up the game and make great changes whenever you want. So, go with the rough draft and flexible plans before finalizing it.***

- ***Polish your researching skills, know what to look for, where to look and how to find the desired information. For that, always keep in mind, not everything you see is straight to the point. Cross check the arguable information and look for the excellent reference before settling down. The resources you use, and kind of information makes a huge impact on the final result, so work on your research skills.***

- ***Add personal touch and be transparent with your audience. Totally professional language in a straight flow, feels monotonous and gives the***

vibe of news. Connecting with readers on the personal level is crucial and it determines the success of the book. So, while writing, try to understand your audience and connect with them, instead of just feeding them with information.

- ***Have a dedicated space for writing. Earlier, I used to think what do i have to do with space, it's just me and thoughts and i can write whatever and wherever I want. But it impacts your creativity and soon, you have to wait for the right mood to write. On the other hand, having a dedicated space always puts you in a mood to write and thoughts just start to come when you sit down and start drafting.***

All the things mentioned above will be discussed in detail throughout the book. At the end, you will get what it takes to write a book. As someone who has authored 4 books and is still counting, I can assure you that you have the ability to write, you just have to work on that. Remember, there will come a time, you deal with the flood of thoughts and also the time when you will struggle to find the best words. But it all comes to an end once you learn to go with the flow.

Lastly, there's no need to pressurize yourself, it is not necessary to learn everything overnight. You have all the weekends, an hour a day and all the time

you spend binge watching stuff and scrolling reels. Learn together with enjoying the process and discover the new aspects of your personality by writing. Let's pick up the pen and paper because soon, you will discover the detailed steps to draft your first book.

Let's Write Well!

- ✓ ***Looking for the ideas***

Selecting a topic that can excite you, add value in others life, looks interesting can be challenging to find, but it's the most crucial part of writing a book. When you find yourself stuck writing about the topics you are not interested in, sooner or later, you will give up. Therefore, selecting the right topic is the key. Whether you are telling a story or writing a book that can teach others, both have to be captivating. Hence, hold your horses and before you start, why not find the best topic? Something trilling for you and your audience!

- ✓ ***What do you mean by a perfect topic?***

There's no definition for the perfect topic and it can be anything that you believe in and want to highlight that topic in front of everyone. Firstly, keep in mind that there are no restrictions, and no rule book says that you have to write about extraordinary things. Prioritize your interests while selecting the

topic and don't let others decide what topic will be perfect for your book.

- ✓ ***What are your dominating thoughts?***

What if I tell you to write about your favorite show, game, your mistakes, or anything you love, surely you can write about that for hours. Similarly, when you select the topic that interests you the most, you can write endlessly. It can be any sport, vacation or your favorite trip, subject, learning you just have to figure that out and see how you can add value in others life with that particular topic. Selecting the topic that always stays with you and makes you curious can not only help you discover more about that topic, but also motivate you to bring out the best information for your readers.

Suppose you recently visited a few historical places in India, and you are interested in knowing more about them, you can start writing about your journey and experiences with additional information and make it your first book.

- ✓ ***Take one step at a time***

There are possibilities that you are interested in multiple things and clueless about what topic should be finalized for your first book. You can start by taking one step at a time and start writing to decide

which topic will be right. Start drafting blogs about the things that interests you, move further with the research. Additionally, when you start writing blogs, you can shortlist the topics and stop researching about the topics that don't interest you anymore. So, take that first step, start writing, be it a story, subject, travel guide, math shortcut, start writing!

- ✓ *Know what is trending*

In a world full of social media, trends, reel and challenges everyone wants to know more about trending things. Trending self-help topics that help people to deal with challenges effectively and make them self-aware can be the topic of your next book. You can mention the things in a more simplified manner with a fresh and new perspective and add your personal views. Moreover, you can write your personal life story, fashion trends, tech trends and other similar things.

Get recommendations from friends and family. Doubting your writing skills in the initial phase is obvious and to overcome that phase, you need to be dedicated and practice consistently to polish your skills. Further, you can show it to your family and friends to get the feedback and work on the feedback to become more confident. Also, you can post it in the parts on your social media handles to know what receives the major response.

Ask your acquaintances what they like reading about the most and what are the problems they are facing, like a survey. Write about that and try coming up with the topics related to that. And trust me, if you research in the right direction, you will find endless things to share together with opinions.

- ✓ ***Write about your upsetting experiences***

We all have similar problems and phases we go through our life; those experiences can be daunting and hard to deal with. So, why not connect with others and write something relatable about all the upsetting experiences you have faced. By writing about upsetting experiences like, dealing with failures, losing someone you love, break-up, make others feel like they are not alone.

Similarly, you also have the option to share your achievements and something you have done in your life to motivate others. It doesn't have to be something grand; it can be everything starting from setting up your business to winning awards in the company you are working from. You can always help others with your personal experiences and also share the mistakes that you want people to avoid.

Whether you are writing about the subject you have specialized in, you are working on the research of some topic you are interested in or even if you are just writing about your personal feelings, gather lots

of information about the subject and add filtered information for your readers.

Follow the above-mentioned suggestions and get the best topics for your first and all the upcoming books. Let's write well!

Chapter-4

Outline and structure of your first book

An outline works like a guide and roadmap which consists of the details about the topics, subtopics, character, theme and plot of the book. When I decide to work on the book, I start to feel overwhelmed with the idea of finishing the whole book within the deadline. Therefore, I give undivided attention and dedicate a couple of hours to make an outline and plan the structure of the book. Also, it gives me direction to keep on writing with the flow together with the hope of completion on time. Now, there are multiple ways to make an outline, but instead of following the methods, just go with the basic outline that you draft and understand without any hiccups.

You already have an underlying idea, but now you want to get into the brief to plan an outline, so start writing the thing in your notepad that you want your book to have. Like, name of the characters, topics to be touched, social messages and concepts to be discussed. Just start writing on your notepad till you run out of ideas. Once you have your raw thoughts, you can start to arrange them and plan the sequence as to what will be discussed at first and how it will end.

Moreover, when it comes to stories, decide whether you want to divide that book into 3-4 parts or you want it to be divided into different chapters with separate names as per the twist and turns. Further, start playing that story in your mind together with keeping the details in mind and developing the settings. First and foremost, note down the starting and ending scenes of 2-3 chapters and what it will look like. Then you can move ahead with the other chapters. Morver, it would be great to keep your outline flexible to edit and make changes for the betterment of the story.

If you are drafting a self-help book or any guide, add as many chapters, topics, subtopics as you can for better readability. As you know there will be no twist and turns so breaking the leanings into parts and subtopics can make it easier for readers to understand. To plan the outline of your non-fiction book, list down the concepts you want to be included into the book. Further, decide the sequence of the chapters and know how you're going to connect them with each other and encourage your readers to move further throughout the book.

In conclusion, you need to specifically give attention and do enough research to come up with an outline to ensure the desired result. But that doesn't necessarily mean it has to be perfect and finalized. You just need an outline for the guidance and starting out, you can always modify it later as per your thoughts and requirements. To share an example with you, when I planned the first outline of this book, only steps were included that too in a precise manner. Further I realized that it can be challenging to make the most out of the pointers and it would be best to add the details. So, here we are!

Pick out a pen and paper and map that outline immediately to commit to that underlying idea of the book!

✓ *How to identify your target audience?*

Once you have the topic in your hand and you are all set to begin the opening sentence of your first book. Stop! Ask yourself, for whom am I writing? Who is most likely to read this book? What will be the age group? What type of words and jargon do I have to use? Who is my 'target audience'? Writing without being aware of your target audience is like trying to hit something without knowing the goal. Suppose if you are drafting a sweet teenage love story then, of course any age group can read this, but your target audience here is the teenagers and college students. Knowing this can help you enhance your vocabulary and make better use of trending jargons together with coming up with dialogues.

Whether you are posting something on social media like any blog post or giving a speech, selling any product or services, identifying your target audience is a must as it increases your chances of success and helps your target audience to find you easily. A target audience is the people who are more likely to read your book because of the preferences

and interests they share. For example, if you have drafted a poetry book or it is like a compilation of poetry and prose, then you should target the individuals interested in poetries and look for the poetry clubs and communities to market your book, because they are your target audience. Off course, you can use creative marketing techniques to highlight your book in front of others too simultaneously.

It is believed to be a common narrative among marketers that 'you can't sell everything to everyone' so, why bother trying? Why not work smart and make some efforts to know who can be the right person? When you know for whom, you are writing, you can feel the connection with them and use relatable things to make it easier for your target audience to understand the concept and follow the story. Further, once people start to read the book, it will bring readers loyalty and you can effortlessly build your readers base for your upcoming titles. Additionally, you can dig deeper about your target audience to make them feel special, it will help you to stand out from the crowd.

Hope you are now aware how crucial it is to identify your target audience before writing the book. So, want to know more about your audience, but feeling clueless?

Don't worry, I have got you covered with the best ways mentioned below.

- ***With the power of the internet and research, you no longer have to spend hours on finding the right surveys and conducting surveys. You get what you want in just a few clicks, so look for the similar books related to your topic, some that are famous and some that are newly published check the reviews, find the related hashtags to find about which age group is attracted by the book. Further, look for the blogs and videos related to that book to get a clear idea about the audience base. As it is your first book and you obviously don't have any feedback and insights, you can try the above method, once you get the insights and reviews, you can refer to them to more appropriate data.***

- ***Explore the genre and know who the right fit for it is. Whether it is thriller, mystery, love-story or life lessons, dig deeper about the books and the authors who have established readers base to get the brief about who can be interested in your story. See, at the end, anyone can read that book as there's no rule book stating that certain books are for certain groups. But when you have an idea about your audience, you can know about their likes, dislikes and challenges, further*** *enhancing the content of your book accordingly. Therefore, you must perform the research to identify the target audience.*

- *Imagine telling golf players to download candy crush and selling cricket bats to soccer players, sounds ridiculous right? So, knowing who is not your target audience is as crucial as knowing who is not. For example, if you are writing a love story for an Indian audience and it is available in India, then you need not market that to hardcore crime fiction lovers and people living in other countries. Also, it would be fruitless to add the elements by keeping them (who is not your target audience) in mind.*

I have no idea what age group you belong to, your gender, community, city or anything else. All I know is that you are an aspiring author who wants to write a book and is looking for all your answers and guidance. So, here I am considering all the basic questions in detail to help you out. So, why not do the same in your first book? Know your readers and write the best you can!

✓ *Polishing the researching skills*

Marvelous researching skills allow you to find the proper answers and use them efficiently in the content you are writing. With proper research, you can gather multiple thoughts surrounding the topic you have selected and then choose the specific facts to include in your book, that are not too specific and not too vague. Also, it offers you the opportunity to filter out the information and explore more about the selected topics.

Now, when it comes to using the power of research while drafting books, different strategies need to be followed for fiction and non-fiction books as per the content requirements.

Also, it would not be the wise decision to include the information you are not sure about and have no expertise in, so, you can clarify the information with the research and avoid the unnecessary arguments. So, let's see how to make your first book extraordinary with excellent research skills.

✓ *Fiction*

You have a story in mind that you can connect with, have experienced before and you want to give words to that story. It is obvious you can't change the emotions and gist of the story. But you can find the best ways to enhance the writing style and dialogue delivery to make the draft relatable and unforgettable.

To enhance the word choice and make the setting of your book look seamlessly relatable, look for the substitute of the words that is under stable for the common audience and sounds more fascinating. With research you will also find that repetition is avoided in the best dialogues, and they are often short and precise. So, do some research about the way of presenting, dialogue delivery and other similar things. Look at as many examples and read as many sentences as you can and work on each and every line of your book to make it memorable.

Additionally, constitute looking for the miscellaneous and different elements to offer your book with the unique touch. Things like, jokes, trending jargons, indirect and manipulative sentences can take your story to the next level. So, once you are done with the outline, dig deeper and move forward in your journey.

- ✓ *Non-fiction*

There is no comparison between nonfiction and fiction, but it is for sure that the research element is more required in the non-fiction books. When you include the results of the famous research and facts, it proves your authenticity in front of the readers and helps you win their trust in no time. So, if you have planned out to write a nonfiction book, sit tight to research for hours to ensure the success of your book.

Suppose you have decided to write about time management, and you will be writing about your personal methods with tips and tricks to help the readers. You might want to add the additional information together with some facts to prove your point and help your readers understand the concept. So, before you start writing about any topic, no matter how much knowledge you possess about that particular subject, looking at some references will be the best decision. Also, you may get to know interesting things while researching. In conclusion, don't try to research all the things together instead go topic wise and break it into pieces to prevent yourself from feeling overwhelmed with all the research.

To polish your research skills, the first thing you have to do is to stop trusting all the sources and get to know the trustworthy sources for the information you need. No matter how true it sounds and how presentable it is, look for the credibility and authenticity of the source before selecting information from it.

Before you start researching it would be great to keep yourself organized and know when to stop researching to prevent yourself from wasting time in unnecessary research. For that, you can list down the questions you need answers for and take one step at a time.

Lastly, it is all about practice and consistently that brings the best fruits and helps you reap the greatest awards. So, be consistent with the research

and slowly you will start to know what source a perfect fit for you and what search is can bring out the best answers.

Chapter-5

Getting to start writing

Dealing with the series of raw thoughts, dozens of new ideas and coming up with new story plots every day, is something writers do through all the time. Although handling the overthinking personality and overwhelming thoughts can become unbearable sometimes, we somehow manage to do it and come up with the best for our readers. Especially for aspiring writers, who work on their passion together with the full-time job, it might be the toughest task to stay consistent with the writing schedule and finish the task within the deadline.

It is unnecessary to mention that we can write anywhere once we have got the written words and inspiration to convey our idea. But we tend to waste hours waiting for that inspiration and mood to start writing. that further leads us to frustration and impact on our motivation to write. Therefore, it is crucial to have a schedule for writing that can remind you about your goals daily and push you forward to achieve those goals.

If you are dedicated toward finishing your first book. Then I bet you have tried before to work on schedule and build a schedule. But you may be struggling to stick to it, because of unrealistic expectations, too strict schedule or any other similar reason. It's effortless to come up with a plan that you can follow daily, but when you come to the action part, you feel defeated as consistency and discipline is not something that you can develop overnight. It takes multiple efforts, daily challenges, and failed attempts to become disciplined.

Creating a schedule and following the right time management techniques makes you more productive and helps you find and stay on the right track. So, with a better schedule you can increase your chances of success and also enhance your writing skills. Also, the main reason we fail to compel our thoughts is because of procrastination. With the schedule and discipline, there will be no room left for procrastination and slowly you will officially author your first novel.

Initially, I used to wait for hours and read multiple books and stuff to inspire me to write and make me feel motivated, but it was not the fruitful thing to follow. Slowly I realized I can go with the flow once I start writing and the thoughts will automatically come. Then, once I started writing with the proper schedule, I used to struggle with the first few words, lines, but after that I found it easy to follow the thoughts and write endlessly. So, hope now you know how important schedules are for writers.

Before we deep dive into how you can create a successful wiring schedule, let's talk about the writing space and how it can drastically impact your schedule. Having a writing space is like a reminder or a zone, which will always motivate you to write and help you gather your thoughts. It doesn't have to be

your personal room or writing studio, it can be a dedicated table and chair that you use when you write. Further, once you have your dedicated writing space, you must respect that space and make rules related to that, like not scrolling reels there or no chatting, it will be just for writing. Even if you have decided to write 200 words in a day, go to that space and leave other things aside, finish that word count, then resume with your day. Moreover, this will allow you to stretch your limits and feel motivated to write daily without any inspiration.

✓ ***Explore further to know how to set a schedule:***

❖ ***Have a goal! Make a realistic and achievable goal without putting too much pressure on yourself. Having goals with deadlines motivates you to work and make you feel confident regarding its completion. So, set your goals and break them into Pisces and know what work count you will complete in a day or in a week. Ensure to keep it flexible and realistic so that you don't feel overwhelmed.***

❖ ***Prioritize! If you continue to think that writing your book is the last important thing for you, you may never be able to complete it. Put writing in your top 5 things if you are serious about it. Make a to-do-list and plan your day by keeping your writing goals in mind.***

- ***Know the right timing! Now, gathering your thoughts, having innovative thoughts, and finding the right words, is not something you can do when you please. If you have decided to write when you are exhausted, you may run out of ideas and feel frustrated. So, make sure to pick the right timing, your most productive time of the day or just do it as the first task.***

- ***Grow with others! If you have friends with the same goals, then it's great, if not, it's time to make some! You can join the writing communities, where you can discuss your work, connect with new aspiring writers who inspire you. Also, you can sign up for the writing workshops and take up some courses. Overall, you must work on your environment to become a successful writer.***

- ***Lastly, kick out the sentences from your mind like. 'I don't write well', 'I will start tomorrow', 'I am not good enough to write a book' Stop! Just start writing! Now is the perfect time to work on your first draft and take one step further. Remember to stay away from all this self-talk as it can impact the way you write. Just be transparent with your audience and write the best you can!***

All the self-doubt you can go though, is obvious in the initial phase, but don't let it stop you or overpower your will to write. By the time you complete

your draft, you start to notice the improvements. So, it is perfectly fine, if your first draft is imperfect. You can work on it again and edit it like a star to get the desired result. Just have some faith and take that first step today to plan a flexible schedule for yourself!

Chapter-6

Writing like a Pro

***C**ontinuing recalling your 'Why' when you walk down the road of challenges is crucial to prevent yourself from quitting. And when you have your 'Why', the reason why you want to write, printed on the screen of your mind, you stay inspired. With the right inspiration, you practice consistently and take your writing skills to the next level. Now, there are various ways to work on your writing skills and know what aspect you need to work on. Firstly, before you start to learn and follow the writing tips I am going to mention in this segment, take a break and attempt to identify where you are lacking.*

Try to know more about your current positions, where you struggle to find the right words or to form the right sentence, or you have noticed multiple grammatical errors in your draft. Continue to re-check and observe mistakes, so that you can work on them further. Once you have your basics clear and you can continue to enhance your skills by using the right tools and different exercises. Like, if you want to add new words in your vocab, look for the synonyms of the most repeated words when you start to write. And, if you struggle to make the chapter outline of the readability of your content is low, use Grammarly and other similar tools to polish up what you have written.

What you are writing is as important as the way you are writing it. It isn't alone the idea that grabs readers attention, it is also about the word choice and the presentation that makes a simple idea remarkable and impactful.

Also, know that the best way to improve your writing is to know what mistakes you've made and what are the shortcomings you have observed. So, step up and start reading your first draft, list down the mistakes you are observing! Explore the below listed tips that will help you enhance your writing skills and elevate your writing game!

- *Shorten the sentences*

  Keeping your sentences crisp and short is the key to grab attention and deliver your ideas in a much effective way. Not all the time, you can express your ideas in short paragraphs as oftentimes there are different things to share. But when you write, eliminate the words like, 'very' 'much' 'more' or any words that makes your sentences wordy and hard to read. Moreover, consider re-reading the sentences to find ways to shorten them.

- *Keep a notepad in hand*

  With multiple things to keep check on, there are chances that you overlook some things. Keep a notepad in hand to list down the ideas you have, feedback and suggestions you receive. By listing down the ideas, you have the opportunity to look back and work on them. Also, you can always turn into that notepad when you struggle to find new ideas.

- ***Be professionals***

You must have noticed that some writers use the childish phases and cliche dialogues to catch the attention of readers. But when you use cliche phrases, it can make you sound unprofessional, which can further impact the mood of the readers. So, go straight to the topic and use direct and short sentences to convey your messages and ideas.

- ***Reach out the readers***

Starting from knowing the mindset of the readers to understanding the challenges they are facing; it is necessary to connect with the readers. Use the right platforms to connect with the readers and know the right questions to ask them. Also, you can also prepare a questionnaire and further you can work on the feedback to improve your skills.

- ***Avoid manipulating the sentence***

Manipulating the sentences means, playing with the words to frame longer and unclear sentences. It is beautiful to play with the words and with the right knowledge, you can get the desired results. But you must know when is the right time to play with the word.

If you are writing a novel, you can experiment more with sentence formation. Further if you are drafting an information-based book. Strictly avoid the indirect sentences and just speak to the point.

- ***Give undivided attention to headlines***

Whatever it is, the title of the book or the heading and even the subheading, its main use is to give readers a rough idea about what's waiting for them. So, giving undivided attention to the headlines is unavoidable. Have a strategy for like a statement or catchy title that describes the topic best. Moreover, try to avoid writing big paragraphs that may make your readers feel bored and add as many headings and subheadings as you can.

- ***Edit like a champ***

As we already discussed, your first draft is going to be imperfect, and it will need further editing. So, read your draft as if you are reading someone else's draft and look for ways to criticize the draft. Work on each sentence and try rewriting it in the best way possible. Also, give yourself time to edit

the draft multiple times before proofreading the last draft.

- ***Get a friend***

  Usually, when I write books, there are multiple writing and editing attempts. So, after a certain point of time it becomes challenging for me to look for the mistakes and quality that can be enhanced. So, I find it the best bet to reach out to a friend who can give me advice without judgment. So, it would be best to ask your friend or any aspiring writers for help, and together work on their suggestions and feedback.

- ***Enroll in courses***

  As we discussed, one of the biggest advantages of writing your book is that you get to work on your self-improvement. So, why not enroll in some courses to work on your skills? There's no need to go for the biggest and most expensive coaching consultation or courses. Start with the research and find a cost-effective course that you can make the most of.

Hope all the above-listed tips will help you to level-up your writing game and successfully finish your first draft. You don't have to accomplish all the

things in a day and apart from that, continue to look for ways to work on your skills.

- ✓ ***Become a reader***

Writing is a continuous roller coaster of the emotions that you have to go through every day. Sometimes, you get overwhelmed with the ideas and find it challenging to deal with all series of thoughts. On the other hand, you face writer's block, where it becomes hard to even draft new words and come up with the ideas. So, to deal with all that, you must read new things and explore the new perspective of looking into things to come up with new ideas. Now, it is understandable that you may want to write about your personal experiences and challenges, but not interested in reading. Not everyone is born a reader, but as there are unlimited advantages of reading, why not give it a try and become a reader?

Remember the days when you hate reading books as a kid and how challenging it was to read something you are not interested in. All the things compiled made your mindset go against the reading habit and you never looked at the reading as a fun experience. Have you ever thought that reading can be adventurous and fun? As an avid reader who reads books in both Hindi and English, I can assure you that if you don't love reading, you are just yet to find the right book.

When you start to read, you allow yourself to explore the new aspect of your personality and introduce yourself to different thoughts and perspectives. Moreover, when you read books, you develop a grasp on the language and learn ways and rhythmic style to give words to your ideas. I know, if you have never picked up or finished a book before that interests you the most, you might be thinking it is easier said than done. So, before you reach a conclusion, let me tell you that reading is like any other habit that you can develop with patience and consistent efforts.

There are many misconceptions and myths revolving around reading and definitions that tell you about the rules of reading. But actually, there's no rule, if you love to read, you are a reader. Then, no matter if you are listening to audiobooks, reading books from kindle, or any genre of your choice. So,

let's make this whole thing easier and explore the tips below that will help you to become a reader!

- ***Get a journal***

  I will advise you to get a reading journal to track down your reading progress, it will work like a reminder. Record all the things starting from the first day of reading to the thoughts that you have while reading. But before writing anything else, write down why you have started reading and keep that purpose clear in your mind.

- ***Start with what you love***

  Have you ever felt bored while talking about your hobby, favorite dramas, and anything that you genuinely like? NO! Similarly, when you read, pick up something that is related to the things you are curious about. Be it sci-fi, astrology, love, poetry, and non-fiction, just keep exploring and you will find the right book for yourself.

- ***Shopping time***

  After the little research, once you have the books you are interested in, it's time to shop. Now, the key is to buy multiple books to increase the no. of pages you are going to read. See, don't be puzzled, when you surround yourself with books, you are

more likely to spend more time with them. Buy multiple books at a time and keep yourself surrounded with books.

- ***Take one step at a time***

Let me tell you something, when I used to buy books in bulk and then kind of felt blue about it when I couldn't read all of them. Also, because I used to set unrealistic goals and try to finish them with in a month. So, remember not to set unrealistic goals and take one step at a time.

- ***Have a schedule***

Having a schedule helps you to be disciplined and consistent. Deciding the reading time for you will help you build a reading habit successfully. Even if you are going to read 5-10 pages a day, decide time for that.

Hope all the above-mentioned things help you to read consistently!

Looking into the details

As an author or soon to be author it is vital for your overall knowledge to know about the multiple genres and how you can work on them. Knowing about the genres will allow you to work smartly and

follow the un-written rules, that may increase the readability of your book and help more people to understand the ideas you are emphasizing on. Not having enough understanding can leave your readers unsatisfied, low book sales and poor reviews on different platforms. Moreover, the audience base for every genre diffres and so their preferences and requirements.

So, overall staying well-informed about how to work on different books can bring different advantages. Getting to know more about Sci-Fi, romance, fantasy, thriller, mystery, contemporary, etc.

The way you pin down the first line of your first book to catch the attention to all the words, phrases, locations, details, everything matters in a fiction book. It is indeed a key to know what to write, but to make things outstanding and novel gripping, you must know what to eliminate.

With the availability of innumerable genres, I can't inform you about all of them. But here, I will certainly help you sharpen your knowledge about all the fiction books and help you write the one that leaves your reader dazzled. Additionally, fiction books require development of plots, sub-plots, characters and lots of imagination. All this needs undivided concentration and creativity. And, if you have been following my journey, you must be aware that I repeatedly worked on fiction books. So, without any

further ado, deep dive into some of the gathered tips listed below.

1. ***Decide the point of view***

I have read some of the fantastic books, but because of the confusions they create, it leaves the readers in a dilemma and impacts their readability, because they are written from multiple point-view without any clarity. So, you must decide whether to narrate the story from a character's point of view or a third person. And, as no rules says you can't merge the both situations, but if you intend to do that divide the chapters accordingly to guide the readers through the story. Suppose, you have narrated one chapter from a character's point of view and then the other from yours, make it a pattern, it is a more enhanced way to be clear.

2. ***Become a creator of the world***

Emerging in novel writing allows you to become creator and lord of your own world, where you control everything. But when you fail to create one, you struggle to come up with creative ideas and that limits your imagination. So, write down the details of the town you imagine and give wings to your fantasies and create your own world, where your story takes place.

3. Get into the details

When I emphasize on the details, I talk about the details in moderation. For the fiction book, you need not to tell what color the photo frame is hanging on the wall, but you cannot miss out on giving a brief idea about the characters' room to help the reader's imagination. So, put yourself in your audience's shoes and write the things they will be pleased to know.

4. Prepare an outline

Believe me you can write the gist of the story in 2 pages and in 200-300 pages, it depends on how you outline it and what details you add. In fiction, the idea of binding yourself with an outline, may sound overwhelming, but it can be advantageous. Outline gives you direction about the story.

To make an outline, decide how your story will proceed, opening incidents you want to talk about in the first chapter and then how you want to take this further in upcoming chapters. Further, you can choose to end the chapter with an incident, dialogue, or day. But try not to end chapters abruptly with pauses. Moreover, you can also divide your books into major parts instead of chapters. Overall, preparing an outline that lets you know where to tell and what to tell is a must.

5. ***Have subplots and hooking scenarios***

I believe you have a great story in your mind, that has a twist and turns or lessons that may impact readers' lives. But readers can't wait for the right part. You have to work on each page of the book and write it in the way that keeps readers going. So, if you are relying on major 2-3 incidents and solely focusing on them, it is good. But it would be great if you add more hooking events and work on the dialogues to create a masterpiece.

6. ***Own your characters***

As an audience, when you feel connected with the characters, you don't want them to change and behave differently, use different language in every upcoming chapter because it feels untrue to believe. Right? So why experiment with their behavior? Work on character development skills, write down the past, language and key qualities of your characters and stick to them unless something big happens in the story. This will help your readers to feel connected and relate with the story.

7. ***Give it great ending***

Why settle for the goodbyes, when you can give a blockbuster, dramatic ending to your story?

While ending the story, find ways to surprise the readers by giving them hints about the next plot, connecting the dots or adding drama in the end. To make a lasting impact, you must work on making the ending of your book memorable. Further this encourages your readers to talk and share about your book, which leads to more book sales and viewership of your book. So, don't forget to work on the ending between the happiness of finishing the book.

Lastly, I advise all fiction writers to never stop learning and keep on fishing for the best ways to make your writing stand out. It can be anything you learn, new words, jargon, jokes, dialogues, use it in your own way, for your book. Moreover, try to talk about the things from different and unheard perspectives to increase your curiosity. This is all for fiction writers, hope now you are up for creating that masterpiece.

✓ ***Working on non-fiction books***

Non-fiction books go beyond the story and the world of imagination and introduce you to new ideas and facts. Also, non-fiction allows you to see the real events through different perspectives. Nevertheless, it would not be possible to make compassion between the genres, as they all have their significance. But it is interesting when you try out and read different genres, like traveling to different cities. Moreover, if you wish to impart your wisdom and educate more people about your business and expertise, writing non-fiction can be the perfect solution for you.

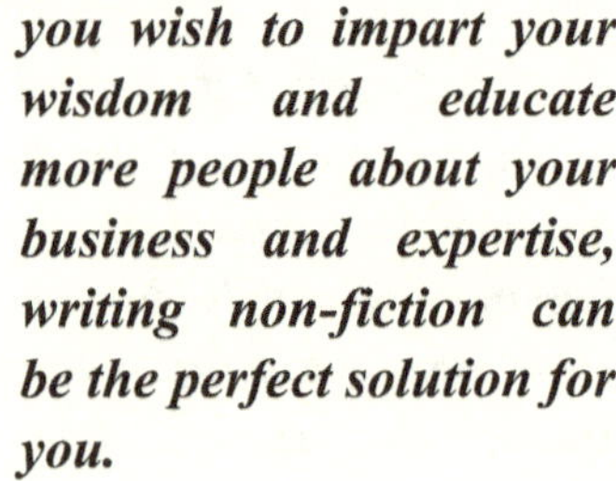

If you are planning to draft a non-fiction book, be specific about the problems you're going to solve or ideas you will talk about. When you include multiple things and ideas in a non-fiction, its purpose stays unfulfilled and leaves your audience confused. So, determine the issues that you will be resolving with your non-fiction book and hold on to the thoughts throughout the book to bring more clarity to the readers. Again, there's no need to wait for the grand idea, you just have to present it with clarity and facts.

Talking about the facts, as you know non-fiction books have a long shelf life because readers use them multiple times. So, you cannot afford to put facts without cross-checking and finding the right source. Avoid including the source you are not sure about. Further, if you want to include the facts, avoid writing the exact numbers and just say 'majority' 'minority' instead.

Now, you have to select the style you plan to follow throughout the book. Suppose, if you want it to be divided in chapters and paragraphs, stick to that or go for small chapters, headings and pointers. Whatever style you select, avoid switching it in between the book. Moreover, as nonfiction books are straightforward, I will strongly suggest you to divide the topics, sub topics and headlines, it increases the readability.

Now, you must work on the introduction, mostly non-fiction and self-help books I read, apart from guides, they have strong and gripping introductions or examples that makes readers go through the entire content. Majorly it shares about the author's personal life story and problems they tackled with or about any famous personality. So, before you work on the introduction.

Trim the information after writing. It is understandable that non-fiction books can be repetitive sometimes because they want to imprint the

solution of the reader's subconscious mind. But if you want to make your book more engaging, read and reread your book and trim the information, you find it unrelated.

Once you are done with the first draft, you feel excited about showing it to others and receive feedback, but that may impact your confidence. Go for at least 2 rounds of self-editing. Here, you have to read your book out loud and edit the things you want to work on, and also work on the correction.

Lastly, work on the title of the book and find the suitable headline of it. Work on the title of the book, once it is finished and you know what exactly it shares. When you select the title that does not match with the information you shared and choose any fancy title, it brings nothing more than confusion.

It may feel like non-fiction books are easier to write, but it is just equal work because of all the research and selection of information that goes into the background. So, I hope you will write like a champ and pin down your non-fiction book successfully with all the above-mentioned and previously mentioned tips. Why wait longer? Go! Begin your research today!

- ✓ ***Knowing more about poetry books***

Are you a poet? Worrying about your growing collection of poetries? Well, as someone who loves expressing my feelings in words. I continue to write more and more poems and always procrastinate when it comes to sorting them out in different categories. Most of the poetries I write are related to my personal suffering, joy, or general life observations.

Now, there are different stages of writing a poetry book, starting from gathering and classifying your poetry collection to writing more poetries to fill up the space, it calls for lots of focus and creativity. When you just write for the sake of writing, you fail to write with charm and add cliches in your poetries. So, let's take a look at what it takes to write a poetry book and how you can finish that.

- ***Know your theme***

  Usually, you may not think too much about the theme while writing. You can write about love, self-awareness, nature, beauty, or death. But when you write in general without dividing the theme, you find it challenging to divide the poetries into different themes. So, it will be your first step for writing a poetry book, knowing your theme.

  Look at the growing collection of your poetries, see what the majority is saying, what are you most interested in, love, friendship, or misery.

Then, decide your theme, you don't have to stick to just one thing, you can divide the sub-theme and divide your book into parts. Remember to choose what interests you the most.

- ***Don't be in hurry***

The happiness that comes from successfully publishing your first book cannot be expressed in words, so you must be excited to finish the draft and get it published. But you can't risk the quality of the connection because of limited time. Also, no one forces you to write the poetries, you should write at your own pace instead of pushing yourself to write more.

Numerous of poetries will be required to finish your first draft, but there will be no point in writing them if it is not your best work or not up to the mark. So, know that you have all the time, and decide to write one-two poetries in a week, write thoughtfully.

- ***Avoid cliches***

Avoiding cliches is all about revising and revisiting your poetries. Before asking for feedback from others, you must give yourself feedback, because honestly, you know what sounds cliche and what is meaningful. So, once

the draft is done, read and re-read your poetries and filter out the poetries you don't like. There will come a time, when you will feel overwhelmed after reading the same things multiple times. So, it would be best to take a break, read some poetry books and then come back to your own draft for editing. Trust me, it is not as complicated as it might sound.

- ***Come back from your comfort zone***

What's a comfort zone in writing poetries and how can you kick out of that comfort zone? When you continue to write about a particular topic with a similar style, it becomes your comfort zone. Then, writing about multiple topics from different views sounds impossible for you. But you must want to add versatility to your book, for your audience and make it perfect. So, come out from your comfort zone and try writing about the different and unfamiliar emotions, something that others may feel uncomfortable to talk about. This way you can polish your writing skills by challenging yourself. Further, it is suggested that you search for the different synonyms available and more sophisticated words to make your book more captivating and relatable.

❖ ***Organize your script***

Are you done with the first draft? How about moving on to organizing your draft. Trying to organize a draft before the completion will bind you to write specific things. Moreover, writing freely will encourage you to express more, without the boundation of topics. Before you have selected the theme and done with the poetries. Now, decide the sequence as per your likings. Start your book with your bestest collection and then divide it in accordance to the sub-theme.

❖ ***Feedback time***

Feedback not only gives you confidence, but it offers you the scope to improve your writing skills and introduces you to the parts which can be worked upon. Feedback games can go wrong when you fail to select the right person that will not hesitate to tell you the truth. When you reach the phase where you will need feedback, know who can be the best person. It doesn't have to be the best-friend or parents, if they know nothing about the poetries. Consider finding the person, who is genuinely interested in poetries and will be delighted to read and offer you with feedback. Further, make changes as per the feedback received. Lastly, try to get feedback from more than one or two individuals.

❖ ***It's time to decide the title***

Initially, I used to work for hours on the title of the book, before moving forward with the draft. But soon I realized, how it can be possible to decide the title with that rough idea, unless it is an autobiography or guide something? It becomes much easier to finalize the title once you are done with the whole book. So, how will you decide the title? Go with these things.

- ***Describe your book in two or three words.***
- ***Keep it classy and elegant.***
- ***Avoid making it complicated by adding difficult words.***
- ***Have a tagline along with the title that says something about your book.***
- ***Lastly, don't do more than 3-4 words.***

❖ ***Think about the publishing***

As a beginner, you might have misconceptions about the publishers and publishing houses. But the publishing system is indeed complicated as it takes luck, Challenges, efforts, patience to get your book traditionally published and lots of funds for the private publishers. But there's one more option left, free self-publishing from kindle. Here, you can publish your book for free and for me it is the best

option for the beginners. You can spend the time and money on spreading the words about your book to increase the sales. It will go out of context if I start to talk about publishing here, but you will get all the answers, just go to the official kindle self-publishing website.

✓ *Mythology*

As people are becoming curious about ancient time stories, history and myths, the popularity of mythological books is rising. Myths are like the stories that have a fundamental role in modern societies. All the mythological tales explain us about the human experience and world. Also, these stories influence the culture and traditions of the society. Also, regardless of all the diversities, language barriers and all the other things, these universal myths bind the human race together. Stories like, after life and good versus evil written by mankind are believable and realistic.

For writing mythological stories, start with a tale you find more believable, and which is deep rooted in every culture.

Now, it's time to give that myth and origin. When you start writing, write about the origin of the myth, history and where it first started. As you know how myths impact human behavior, so they must be ages ago. It can't be possible as myths started yesterday can impact the world. So, write about how

they started and fabricated and how they become what they are today.

Whatever, myth tale you want to write, no matter how illogical and silly it sounds, if it has something to do with everyone's daily life, chances are that you will create a masterpiece for your readers. So, make your mythological tale relatable and give it a trending touch and make it captivating for your readers.

Create a villain and hero for your stories. Develop the character of the hero, which is admirable and lovable, smart, and super intelligent, like most of the fantasy world heroes. Also, strong characters are remembered for days and years and impact the personality of the readers. If it's your first time writing a mythological fiction, avoid making general assumptions and know what is being accepted out there. Like, characters with supernatural powers, relatable struggles, and inspiring life. On the other hand, villains need to be realistic as well with proper motives and challenges.

Lastly, you don't have to do everything on your own, you can borrow and take inspiration from what's already in there. Like, ages old mythological tales from your point of view with extra details. Also, myths are not copyrighted and that's what makes them best, you can write or experiment almost

everything with them, it is only limited by your imagination.

So, spread your wings and write your best. With right practice and proper research, you become unstoppable. Be it fiction, non-fiction, poetry or mythology, mystery, it takes courage and an optimistic attitude to come forward and present your thoughts in the best manner, in front of the world. So, why worry about the results and feedback, just enjoy the process, and take this opportunity to improve yourself, and your writing skills. Lastly, I encourage you to take that first step today, before you move on with the thoughts and start pinning down your first draft. Let's write your best!

- ✓ ***Cookbooks & Travel Guide and other informative books***

Informative books that have nothing to do with the fictional world, ideas, or imagination can be challenging to write. Whether you want to write travel diaries, cookbooks, academic guides, or any other book that has informative content, you can't really add on much apart from your personal experience and a different point of views. So, all you can do is to try your best and work on the best and fun ways to present the information. Also, I find it a misconception among us that informative books make us bored, and they have nothing exciting to share. But these books played a major role in my life, and they

helped me explore more about architectural wonders, customs, traditions, foreign cultures, and natural beauties. Hence, I still believe these books hold immense power and influence. So, I will cut it short and sum up what Ihave to tell you in few bullets:

- ***Plan the structure of the book with proper steps. Like, plan parts, then index, chapters, subheads, and minor headings. Break the book into as many chapters as you can and have a proper chapter outline, short paragraphs and multiple headings. Whatever topic you have decided, once you are done with the research, break down the topics, chapters before you start writing. Also, as guides are supposed to teach people about and make them familiar with the places. So, consider adding notes at the end of the chapter.***

- ***Keep chapters as short as you can. Avoid stretching the information and adding useless information to your guide. Also, give proper heading to the information, so the reader doesn't have to browse through the whole book to find the information.***

- ***Include a few pictures and your real-life examples. Any picture can be inserted with the source that looks suitable.***

- ***Watch your facts and mention the source of the facts if they are not famous and known. Moreover, avoid the facts you are unsure about. As they can make readers confused, impacting the purpose of the book.***

- ***As the more is merrier, it would be great if you can co-author a book with someone and get help in writing your guide. So, connect with someone who is interested and shares the same interest.***

Holding your book in your hands will be like a dream and you will love the whole experience. So, don't give any second thoughts to this and whatever you want to write, start working on that.

Chapter-6

How to Edit Like a Pro?

The whole journey of writing a book is unfinished without editing it carefully and eliminating the chances of second doubts.

Although, as an author, it's compulsory to get your book edited by a professional editor. But you cannot be sure about your writing without one or two rounds of self-editing. Self-editing can take more time than usual, but it results in perfection and helps you get the desired results. Moreover, you know there will be few rounds of editing so, don't limit your creativity trying to write the perfect first draft.

There are some apps that help you to run the grammar and spelling checks. And that's the round number of one the editing. Follow simple steps and select one part at a time for the editing. In the first round, run your content on grammar check apps and search closely for spelling, pronunciation, and other small grammatical mistakes.

Remove the parts that readers will skip. While you are at the second round of proofreading, don't give any attention to the big mistakes and focus on the paragraphs. Read through the chapters again and look for the parts that can be trimmed. Just after treading once, you will realize, some parts are exaggerated and they can be trimmed. So, why not cut it short?

After writing for years, I have noticed that there are some words I tend to overuse. And it becomes a habit and over time, you may find it daunting to deal with. But as the proofreading gives you an option to eliminate these words, why not start it? Try replacing the overused words with the synonyms. Try replacing the maximum words, but don't overburden yourself by trying to replace all of them.

When you exhaust yourself from reading the same content repeatedly, you can't edit brilliantly and skip crucial things. So, I suggest you put the draft aside for a week and take a break. You will be refreshed and see things differently after a few days. After days, you will definitely forget what you wrote and will be able to correct the mistakes.

Now, let me introduce you to the technique that I personally prefer. I prefer to read things out loud and also try to listen to it from someone's voice. So, I take help from google assistant and listen to the words I wrote days ago. It helps me know where exactly I went wrong and how I can work on that.

Lastly, there's one thing that I can add, never over-do the editing. No matter how many times you edit, this series rounds will never end, and you can get stuck in that. If you are sending your book to a professional editor, don't forget to read it thoroughly before moving on to the publishing round. So, know

when to end the series of editing and declare your draft ready to be published.

Chapter-7

It's time Guy's

I am truly grateful as you have completed this book and proud to see your dedication toward your passion. All I can say is that, follow the listed advice and tips, to complete your first draft and forget about the publishing, it can also be managed effortlessly once you have your draft in hand.

You may not author the best-seller book in the first step of your journey, but with the consistency in your thoughts and actions, you can surely touch the heights of your writing career and author a best-selling title.

Continue to motivate yourself and make all the efforts, increase your viewership, visibility, connect with fellow authors, make social media accounts, post regularly and do all the things that will push you closer to your goal.

Be clear and dedicated toward your vision and you can see the success coming to you!

Start your journey today!

About My Books:

Saahi '&' Sudheer

"Saahi '&' Sudheer" is a novel based on friendship, attraction, and love. The novel relates to all generations with their time, life, and story. It is a cute story in which Saahi and Sudheer were childhood friends; Sudheer was an artist and Saahi was a writer. When Saahi came into Sudheer's life, he felt a lot of change. Both were good friends, but after some time, Sudheer and Saahi both realized they loved each other, but it was too late. Now, what will happen? Will they meet? Will they express their love? Will painting and writing affect their life? There are so many questions, and for the answers, you have to read the novel "Saahi '&' Sudheer". The novel includes many sentiments, emotions, and feelings that one can easily relate to in their daily lives. It also includes many ups and downs in school life, friendship, and separation, making everyone think about what will happen now.

The story of 'Diya' is inspired by a true incident. The story discloses all the rituals of society, which we have to follow without any objection. Diya didn't speak a single word against dominance. She felt abused and hated herself. What happens next? Does she make a voice against her husband and society? What will happen to her? What will happen in her life? Let's come and join the journey of Diya's life!

"Post Card" Every life has a lesson

The book contains a collection of true, inspiring stories. The idea for creating this book came from our busy and stressful lives, where there is a need to inspire everyone. The author wants this "inspirational book" (post card) to reach everyone, as every story in this book will inspire you. It provides life lessons and shows how much you have been affected by your life, and how many of you can influence others through the lessons you have learned. The book includes many authors, aged between 17 to 42 years, who have learned valuable lessons from their lives and now want to inspire you.

After reading this book, you will be motivated and able to do something good in your life.

"When we entered 2020 happily, we never knew that in the coming few months we would be imprisoned in our homes under the name of lockdown due to the pandemic.

"Cooker Ki Seeti" is a compilation of 6 plays based on the lockdown. The lockdown has been a tough phase for all of us, where we were not allowed to go anywhere. We were forced to stay at home and experienced new things. We spent quality time with our family members, laughed and cried, dealt with separation and problems, had schools remain closed, worked from home, and saw workers return home, while children could not visit their grandmothers' houses. Some marriages broke up, and we started living in a digital world. Social media played an important role in our lives. This book is an account of all these experiences."

"Gulmohar" is a poetic masterpiece that invites readers to explore life through a unique and enchanting perspective. With the eloquence of a poet's soul, the author paints a vivid picture of existence, likening it to the serene mountains, cool breezes, boundless skies, innocent childhood, carefree birds in flight, and the vibrant colors of a rainbow. In this compilation of poems, the essence of life is poured into words to make an impact in your life.

The book "Gulmohar" is a treasure trove of verses that highlights the beauty of life's every hue. You'll find yourself immersed in a world where each poem resonates with the promise of a brighter tomorrow. The author's words are like a fragrant breeze that gently wafts through your soul, carrying with them the essence of hope, resilience, and the celebration of life.

Grab your copy now!

Contact the Author:

Website: yogitawarde.in

Email: Authoryogitawarde@gmail.com

Team@yogitawarde.in

Instagram: author.yogitawarde

Twitter: @wardyogi

LinkedIn: yogita warde

Facebook: Author Yogita Warde

www.ingramcontent.com/pod-product-compliance
Lightning Source LLC
LaVergne TN
LVHW091038150826
845672LV00006BA/1875